Passion and Grace

The
Photography and Poetry
of Gordon Fox Kreplin

ISBN: 978-1-09837-934-6
Ascencion Recordings , Inc.
First Edition.
www.gordonkreplin.com

Acknowledgments

Special thanks to:

Ellen Holder and Jocelyn Coverdale for assistance in editing this manuscript, Beth Hewett at Defend and Publish for coaching, Jon and Erika Pescevich for advice on design and intent, Joy Moses-Hall, Ph.D., who stunningly advised me to "crash the white space!" and make the photos larger, Dr. Rick Trummer for guidance in the use of *InDesign*, Fr. Phil Glick for his careful reading of this manuscript and for his encouragement throughout its creation.

Last but not least, and perhaps most, to my wife Cathy, who tolerates my incredibly bad jokes and periodic ranting about art, spirituality, and politics.

Formatting and cover design by Ascencion Recordings, Inc.
Author photo by Pat Hansen.

Forward

Gordon Kreplin and I met after worship one Sunday morning when he commented on my sermon. His were not the usual words, "Good sermon, Padre." It was clear that he had listened deeply for meaning and was ready to plumb for more.

As a parish priest, now retired from active ministry and having served as a military chaplain with two deployments to combat zones, I've learned that God's grace comes at unexpected times and in unexpected places. If my eyes are open and my heart is tuned, I can sometimes catch a glimpse of Ultimate Reality breaking in.

Gordon's eyes and heart are so tuned. He can behold beauty while others may pass it by without notice. His heart is tuned to the rhythm and lyricism of creation so often go unheard. His poetry and photographs are expressions of God's grace being revealed in this world.

As a child, Gordon watched his father, a solar physicist and amateur photographer, develop photographs in the dark room. Images, both light and dark, emerged on paper as if by magic. He learned to look not merely for things seen, but for those things unseen, that which we call eternal.

Gordon is an award winning photographer. He was an affiliate of The Professional Photographers of America and has judged national and international competitions. His work has been exhibited in numerous galleries on the Outer Banks of North Carolina where he and his wife Cathy reside.

Gordon is a classically trained musician. He studied guitar under John Marlow at American University and with José Tomás at the Óscar Esplá Conservatory in Alicante, Spain. He is a performance artist who has taught and toured nationally and internationally.

His poetry and photography pulse with the rhythm of life and love. This rhythm is nothing less than passion. Images of light and darkness continue to emerge as if by magic. This is sheer grace.

Peruse this book with a casual eye and where you catch a glimpse of grace breaking into the mundane or you feel the pulse of a passionate rhythm, pause; take it in, enjoy. I did, and I think you will too.

The Rev. Phillip R. Glick
Episcopal priest and Army National Guard chaplain, retired.

Artist Preface

This book is about revelation. Discovery of self, of others, of beauty seen and unseen, of grace and compassion. It has some structure but not a formal presentation by chapter and verse. It is meant for the reader to wander a bit with no real agenda other than that of embracing a view of the world as reflected in life experience.

Just as revelation seemingly has no format and can occur quite randomly, so God's words come to us in those silent spaces, those thin places, through the veil, and reveal a process of the "Thou," a place or relationship, or non-relationship, so described by theologian Martin Buber.

This revelation has been, for me, comprised of many endings that are beginnings. Life and love are random. Let us reach out and touch beauty while we can, and allow that beauty to embrace us in return. For me, there is a master carpenter whose design is a part of this heart's journey.

GFK

Images of sound, color and time wash through
memory and feeling to become
pattern's awareness of future dreams.

May the depth of metaphor embrace in spirit belief and lighted path!

On Creativity

Let the abstract flow as a gentle tide
In the comfort of "unknowing."
May the depth of metaphor embrace
In spirit belief and lighted path!

Creativity, the spark of muse,
Where one discovers the doing,
Purpose and passion is to become
An extended grace of knowing.

Ponder these lines that follow –
My hope is that themes detect
Crystalline melodies of grace and flow,
We to greater purpose reflect.

February 9, 2021   Outer Banks NC

Beauty's Intent

Passion each note rings clear
Greater harmony crescendos appear.
Vibration, focus, beauty of sound
In Thy presence gifts abound.

Vision, this beauty timeless revealed
Truth transcendent, my spirit healed.
Concert communion thy beauty mine –
Worldly fortune – what place or time?

From darkness to light I ask reprieve,
Art for art's sake now to leave.
Success, still beauty, timeless to might,
Grant this vision be given sight!

October 10, 1989   Fort Washington MD

In This Space Known

In this space known
familiar feelings surround,
yet are distant memory.
Strange, alone,
Their return hardly notices
my present state.

Existing outside awareness
their power is proportion
to perceived reality ...
Ultimate truth lies just beyond.
I reach out, its path illusive, kinetic;
changing in shape, form,
color, awareness;
Transforming, transcending,
Altering not in substance.

My search is for Oneness
 Of Heart,
 Of Mind,
 Of Spirit ...

March 1989   Washington DC

Dream Time

Paradox of time and values,
a yearning for lost youth
listening to oldies and New Age music;
Our generation wonders
"Where have all the flowers gone?"

Carole King cries softly
to lost hearts and dreams,
Traveling under logos
BMW, Mercedes, and Volvo ...

Bands in Dream Time,
values lost to greed.
Silent cries from within
stir Upwardly Mobiles
to remember ...
A time of caring, a desire for peace.

A collective subconscious
confuses our awareness.
Revealed in melancholic pangs,
it shrouds itself in a convenience
of comfortable prejudice.

It's a "long time passing ..."

September 1990   Washington DC

Emerald Sequence

Chasing rainbows, sequencing of dreams
(alternative journeys
in the passions of women)
Seed to grasses green flowing,
mindful opulence to summer serenity.
The many seasons of my life,
swiftly searing soaring beaming,
in forward motion of motionless time.
Stopping, softly caressing to consider,
sensual sequences singing
brightly in my memory.
Smoothly softly, sweetly smelling
Graceful arching in passion posed.
Plans piercing burning
this time sequence now.
To creative purpose!
Senses demure, I listen
and search for a voice interior
to align myself with a greater Plan.

1989 Rocky Mount NC

Night Scene Arboreal

The street light shines through your branches,
imposing the city upon gentle green.
Breeze, cool and sallow,
washes through my consciousness.
Leaves flutter, a language murmured
of Romance and Adventure.
Rooted in memories, vibrations,
this essence – neither smell nor taste, yet both –
Touches imagination.
A Destiny yet to be perceived
Within so many avenues tried,
like branches reaching to awareness ...
Becoming one with sallow breeze,
my passions draw inward to your destiny.

September 8, 1990   Washington DC

This Passage Time

Time's passage prickling, pouring,
pulling memories to crossroads.
Passions perceived of visions
unfulfilled by present realities,
so thought of in contexts
known, yet hidden by shadows,
fears that time passes
unconcerned
with centered need.

So many vibrations,
reflections of Spirit,
in those I have loved
or in those received.

Like a traveler steeped
In journeys of the heart,
One point, one part
to that different drum
I follow as one.

Alone here now
I am to become,
in journals interior
this passage I keep,
noting time's pace,
there is much yet to seek.

To release this gypsy life
Is to me an intrigue.
In heart pieces mine,
of this passage time.

October 7, 1990   Washington DC

These Yesterdays Seem Shadows

These yesterdays seem shadows
of dreams that never were ...
I hold to hopes past
and confuse them with reality.
Your promises echo like
shouts in my memory,
broken to the core.
Driven like dark clouds in tempest,
they bring pain and confusion.
"Why" is answered in silence.
Like a lead-filled cavity,
it leaves only acrid taste,
and still there is the silence.

October 1994 Washington DC

Time Transfer

Transcendence transistor,
Electric time pass to phase final,
Mode shift to spirit seek ...
Freedom to struggle again.

Passage to light, Merciful Angels,
give us this day our daily ...
Cares of time space,
Which place is left to those behind?

Redemption, caring to risk,
Memorials not of stone
but actions of giving.
Caress of Spirit Vessel,
Time belongs to God,
Eternity to the living.

Light plane shine through
to this dimension place.
Cracks, streaks, illumination seeks,
lifting covers of darkness ...

Transfer time,
God, Love, Light –
Grant us strength and peace.

July 1988 Nashville NC

Memories and friendship, from one place of grace to another . . . .

How else do we learn to love?

Camaro Madness

Sex flash six
cylinders or more,
or less,
depending on point of view.
Sixteen, a perfect "Ten"
plus six,
or twenty minus four.

Miles per gallon
or day or week.
Automatic,
or four on the floor?
Mag Wheels a destiny
to Freedom or Flight?

Destination Breathless,
which road is true?
Gain wisdom in the journey
and remember,
it's up to you!

For Johnny, Happy Birthday!
December 10, 1984   Rocky Mount NC

Crystal Linda

Billowing sails heart-shaped to face,
breath blown Divine Love's lasting embrace.
Your spirit vibration journeys forth
through seas interior west and north.

Your passions singing, numerically ringing,
create harmonies yet to be drawn;
Your childlike wonder of mysteries sown
is to me infectious, this essence known.

Each sun rising shimmer in your eyes
refracts like crystals color spectrum-wise;
Perception illuminating gifts to call,
expression of power, sends light to all.

Discoveries await you, refined matrix to place,
shape's progress defined, reflects this inner space;
The patterns are drawn within you no doubt,
to solve first the puzzle is to find them without.

Outlined through your will and God's grace,
this structure's solution will be your embrace;
May all the softness you hold to share
be ever returned to you in full care!

December 6, 1990 Washington DC
For Linda, my crystallographer friend
who lit up a jellyfish!

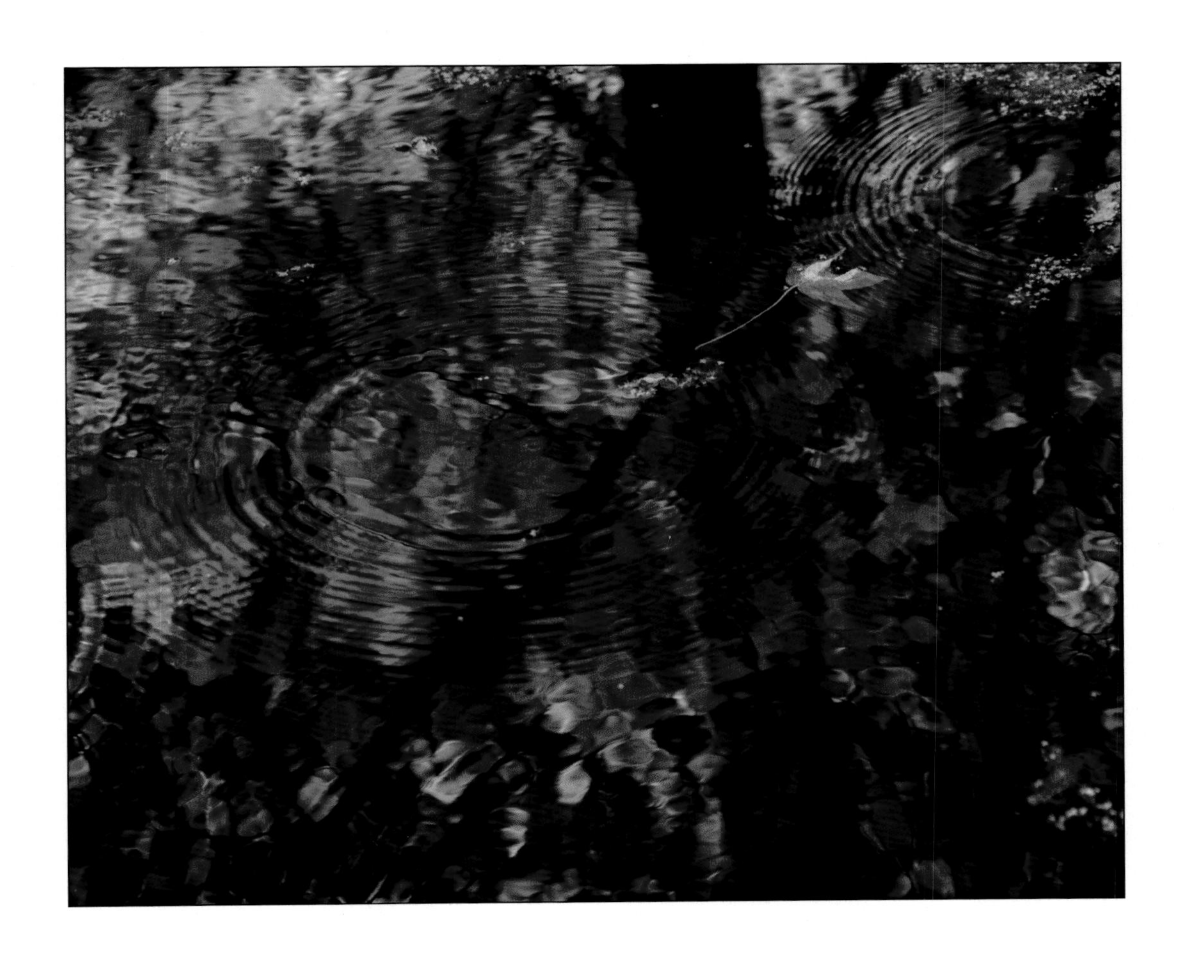

The Lie

Desire so deep, unmet,
longing fulfillment of simple promise,
Child made, this desire gathers not.
A vapid echo of
life's unnamed teacher,
asleep to muse of present tense.

Dreams of oneness so intense,
this pain rushes, fills
a place reserved for joy,
Wrenching like abrasive,
on skin, tenderly awaiting,
It grates upon this holy space.

This promise, never spoken,
but made, nonetheless,
walking wavering wondering,
a promise so simple, love,
an innocence broken.

Creative images spoken not,
send gentle muse silent ...
How to heal
without bitterness
this blemishing scar?
Cynicism the lasting flaw,
promises of childhood casting far;
Can they be never law?

O Muse return,
soothe this spirit ache, brood ...
Bring images, sounds, colors,
of hopeful joy to allude,
Beauty to resound, reshape, resend,
rebuild to grace unbound.
This fervent prayer, so gentle in shape,
Hear and allow,
Hopeful envoy of beauty now.

October 1980 Arlington VA

Crystal Promises

Crystal promises keeping
Sensitive eyes green weeping
The glass palace is shattered, broken –
Hope's vision in disarray was spoken.

To no avail was the awful reply,
Love's chambers interior now surely die.
The once many moods in pieces fly –
Away to lands seen never again.

Tears like diamonds, angular fall
Essence crystalline, powerful yet small
Reveal a past so quickly formed –
Love's venture so successfully scorned.

To live, loving yet another day
Completes this tragic, comedic play.
Love's nest hope dreams, a book now closed –
Experience gathered, life essence flows.

November 17, 1990 Washington DC
Upon a mother's passing

Marcel

Aching, senseless stricken,
Marcel in AIDS final lay.
Wrist upon forehead wrested,
Eyes blinded, he saw only pain.
His vision was for passage,
deliverance from this plane.
I played guitar for him,
A Priest came in to pray.
Hello Marcel, he softly toned,
God's blessing I'll give you today.

Listen to a lullaby, Father gently spoke,
I'll anoint you with oil graced.
Marcel replied ever so faintly ...
But my friends, they wait,
I have to leave –
(this end, Marcel with trouble faced)
We love you here, we want you to stay,
the priest replied in caress.
He held his hand and stroked his arm;
Marcel he blessed.

And so with prayer
my guitar echoed a serenade.
A lyric wave, a warmth, a power –
He was in the room
His Spirit revealed,
a oneness flowered.

There He promised to be,
(where gathered are two or three)
And this day in His name,
We became transcendent, free.

October 4, 1990 Washington DC
For Father Brian, Chaplain, Gift of Peace

In Repose of Evening Sun

In repose of evening sun,
an ocean breeze, a summer porch,
preludes to different paths
served our purpose as one.
Laura Nyro seemed a goddess,
speaking to lost hearts,
finding comfort in summer adventure
that would for a lifetime last.

Lost melodies sing of past hopes
now present but still unknown,
still waiting, watching, hoping ...
Distant beach days guarded
Future remembrance of salt, sun,
Burned into the souls of our becoming –
Finding, needing.

At sixteen I saw Death –
You were there.
It was blue, still, and did not breathe,
    and it took away our innocence.
I can reach back on waves of melodic
response and smell the crowd
on twenty third street.
"Keep back!" I shouted
to no avail, waving my signal flags,
as you felt for a pulse ...

And later the Captain called,
"Was that guy breathing
    when he left the beach?!"
      " I think so," was my timid reply.
(after all, I was sixteen)
"Well he ain't breathin' now!"
the Captain shouted.
And the line went dead.

I climbed back up to continue
a watchful vigilance
from the vacuum of my perception.
And the only constant was
a summer porch, an ocean breeze
in repose of evening sun,
and the intimacy of experience shared.

A call came for you that summer
of news that your father went beyond.
I watched as you left for home and somehow
knew a little more innocence was lost.
And through the pain of wisdom,
there was still the porch
looking out into the ocean night –
you could almost touch the future;
A blanket of melancholic dreams,

Of places yet to be seen
Melodies yet to be heard
Of romances yet to be won and lost ...
Our summer porch in nightfall watch
held a tenderness, impassioned
in repose of life-death concerns.
We respond with uncertainty
while memories past
propel us into future cares.

And still there is that summer porch
An ocean breeze
And my closest friend.

April 2, 1997 Elizabeth City NC
For Bruce

The Guardian
NAGS HEAD
LIFEGUARD ON DUTY
H2O TEMP.
HIGH TIDE
LOW TIDE
SURF COND.
ADVISORIES
RED FLAG INDICATES
BEACHES CLOSED TO SWIMMING

Christmas, always, each year arrives. But Where is Santa?

Innocence lost ... but a lifetime of hope.

Christmas and being only Six

The tender age of six
before the arrival of siblings,
before the loss of safety and innocence.
Riding in the back of our '57 green Chevy,
a journey to Christmas Eve at St. John's
a country church of Colonial Era.
The stained-glass window behind altar
awaiting all,
a hopeful envoy of yearly grace.
"Are we there yet?" was my question,
a very big question;
at least to one of only six,
anticipation filled ...

It snowed
snowed
snowed on that Christmas Eve.
Stopping at roadside Dad took chains from the trunk,
and magically placed them on our wheels of green-shaded sleigh
to begin our pilgrimage anew,

"Are we there yet?"

The sound of those spiraling chariot wings
were silent yet crunchy,
as our transport followed
the narrow snow-packed lanes
of country road, a highway called Indian.
Soon to be four lanes of confusion and progress.

Imagination ran high, seeing only snow sheets
descending upon Our Christmas Cocoon.
Head lifted from rear seat of chariot, an exclamation!

"Are we there yet?"

A magical view of the world as it passed by.
Many thoughts of Santa and his visit.
Would we be home in time?
Would he leave if we weren't asleep?
Would he eat the cookies on the hearth?

"Are we there yet?"

December 25, 2020
Outer Banks NC

4.80
4.30
4.50
4.30
4.30

Christmas Rap

Christmas tide, pain's sweat tears
drop one by one into oceans wide.
Yule time's bride begets commercial tide
sweeping senses in singular pride.
A wave of selling surface emotion,
merchants beguile us
in sensate promotion.

Family, friends we cherish most,
around tree trimmed finds
to which do we toast?
Our values, strayed and so amiss
in season's celebration, eternal bliss?

To you Lord, I finally cry!
There is so much doubt –
what reason, why?
For us now, your Son was born,
a time to rejoice, not be forlorn.

Through tender tears
are glimpses now and then,
That speak of joy, goodwill towards men.
Yet this message is so hard to see
amidst Christmas dollars' endless valley.

Avarice becomes pride's utmost folly
in fa-la-laughing season's jolly,
Perhaps the waiting hurts the most –
these presents embody not the host.
They hide impatience
with world concerns,
an inside-outside sharing that burns.

True gifts symbolic
this essence fine,
To turn back the "shoulds"
will heal this wrap
In Christmas time.

December 1990 Washington DC

Christmas Song of Sadness Seeking

All things that could have been
this Christmas fall away.
To the child within,
hope's dreams and fears
come together in one play.
Like gentle snow in spirit cleansed,
a whitened sadness, this heart
today finds new hope our King.

This sadness pride though torn of love,
constricts the stream of light above.
Grace flows from springs so clear
that each Noel season appear.
I can't deny your love for me,
in Christ you came, our heart's journey.
To lead us in faith's hope renewed,
Your gift received, our spirit imbued.

You so loved the world,
Your son endured
great pain and suffering
to cleans sins obscured.
It's through this gift that You appeared
to guide us walk in faith not fear.

Grant that my love will not stray
and that I live through You each day.
For doubts of Your place in my heart,
forgive;
and with gentle grace
lead in present start.
From this rebirth,
new strength and courage
will then begin.

All things of beauty come to pass,
hope's faith renewed, a half-filled glass.
And should I ever again complain
this life is much too filled with pain,
I shall see anew my savior clear –
reborn again this midnight, dear!

December 15, 1990 Washington DC

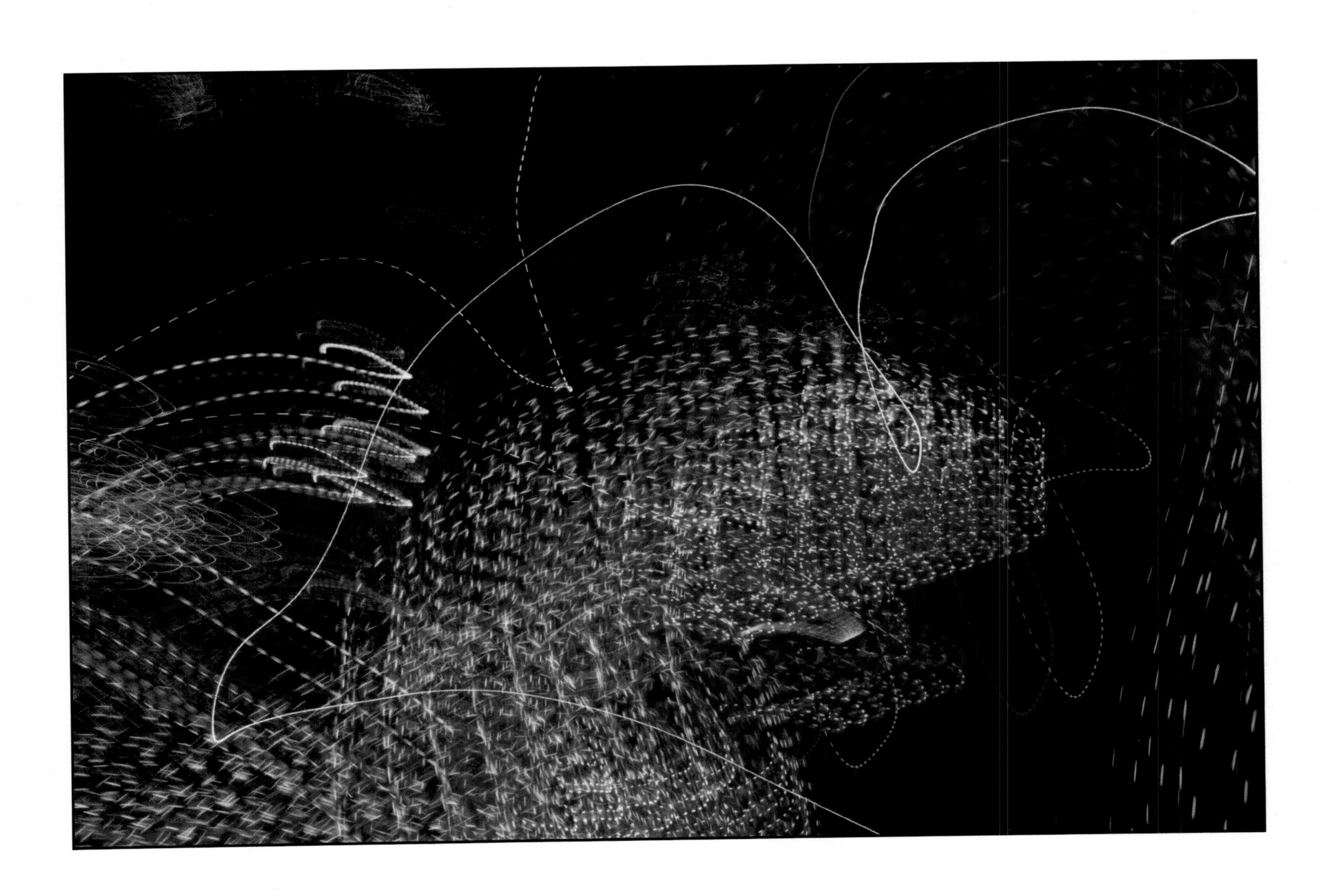

Image of Christmas Past

Silent Night, our final hymn and prayer,
our old country church, St John's ...
Families, illuminated by rows of gentle
candlelight, lifting song, love, sadness and hope –
Echoing in the decorated arches of curved ceiling,
our colonial majesty.

Scent of fresh pine,
incense floating –
As though a blanket of hope.
Drifting, sensing, cleansing ...
reflections of past and future,
expectations of Gift, again to be received,
offered in yet another act of grace;
God so loved the world.

We would see again
that sacrifice of giving and love,
bringing the meaning of this day
in time with Alpha and Omega.

A cross would come –
Ascendance of spirit, bathing eternal,
A manger to trade for Calvary and above,
Two sides of one coin;
A first and last love.
A light that is seen yet hidden,
A light that can blind with grace,
A light of sadness and joy ...

This image of candle and song
aches in memory of you, my sisters,
singing with gentle tear
somehow knowing that all was not well.
And yet, this feeling so intense,
would not cause hope to cease.

This to me is the meaning.
Savior did not come
because all was well;
He so loved the world and gave –
That we might become
a candle of faith and love to tell ...

December 25, 2020   Kill Devil Hills NC

Morning Glory

Are images of Beauty our own creation? Are we available to the Other, the painter, the poet and composer of truths universal?

Celestial Winters Wandering

Sun sparkles shine
upon fields crystalline, snow
As small diamonds refine
patterns of forward time.
Sensuous soaring delights,
texture's embrace refined
sound reflections flying
a color's moods sighing.
Celestina, bells in harmony
brightness vivid forming,
my imagination wonders,
winding possibilities ...
Wistful, winsome, seeking
Celestial Winters Wandering!

November 16, 1990   Washington DC

Feeling's Pattern

Morning spoken softly,
whispered of your touch.
It washed through
my first awareness
in presentness embraced.
A gift unveiled, thoughts glisten.
A centered faith unspoken,
An essence now vision
known only to become.

Revealed yet undefined,
a passage of two hearts,
Through spaces full but silent,
Faith's journey, hope, is found.
This flower's gentle fragrance
silky, sweetly, scented,
seen of golden patterns
draws near to my embrace.

Yet never can I hold it
merely to my mind its grace
will blossom in my spirit,
and blend our hearts as one.
This gift then seems so likely
that we separately become
one vision shining brightly –
Feeling's pattern, now begun.

March 7, 1991 Washington DC

Gift

Shared sunlight
Floating
Spirits melting
Transcending ...

Seeing our humanity we flew ...
no longer man or woman,
corporeal in past reflection –
An embrace.

Brief moment stopping time,
lifted by a cloud ...
Tears of joy unknown,
and awareness that you were there.

This gift was for two.

October 1, 1983   Nashville NC

Time's Response

Your embrace, gentle touch, and kiss
are familiar yet unknown.
Swirling in my memory,
your scent lingers in closeness.
A wave, a vibration,
a welcomed intrusion of awareness ...
Was there a connection?
Remembrance of days past
leaves not details, but essence.
Within this essence,
a future longing
for memories yet to see ...
I patiently await time's hopeful response
of future dreams to be.

February 19, 1991 Somewhere out there

Wedding Song

Hand outstretched
Wings graced, hope and peace,
Union of gifts
that two spirits become.

Green breeze gilded
smells sweetly in time.
Essence sensuous
create what is thine!

May beauty and faith
from this union flower.
A light shining outward
to those then empowered.

Whether daughter or son,
may God's grace flow within.
Peace to you both
your spirits now one!

1987 Rocky Mount NC

Oriental Dance

Sultans flashing, harems dancing,
veils flowing rhythmic, Call.

Beauty, hidden sensual,
crescent scents of incense
Illusions shadow movement,
suggesting lands not far.
Moorish passions arching
(red ruby's navel intensity)

Swaying lithely –
Melodious rattle of sequins,
in sequence to sensations formed.

Patterns
(passions awareness)
Weave harmonies yet mysterious,
To Arabia!

A thousand nights call
this oriental dance,
Zambra Granadina!

November 16, 1990 Huntington WV
To Issac (Albeniz)

The people who sit in darkness have seen a great light;
for those living in a land overshadowed by
death, light has arisen.

Mt 4:16

Shining Man

Walking man in city's heart,
A shining sun, crisp breeze clean;
Mirror images hint rebirth
In reflecting pools of emptiness.

Monuments of values human,
green greed overgrown gone;
Geese gaggle near water's edge
and hiss as man goes by.

His search for meaning
In this city of capitol,
Is punctuated, bitten foully;
A headline reads,
(in a Post called Washington)
Man Goosed by Reflecting Pool!

September 16, 1990   Washington DC

Starry Eyes

Mx B1
H and A
Bombs...
Moral Moral
Majority Right
Wings of Hope
dashed...
Mushroom Mushroom
Happy Mushroom
Cinderella, starry eyes
gone, gone...

December 3, 1990   Rocky Mount NC

Veils of Truth or Darkness

This truth hidden ...
folds of a curtain of darkness,
cover light and awareness
of all perceived reality.
Attempt to uncurl unfold take down
to purpose of clarity,
this fabric has great resistance
in this reality, semi-awake;
Like a lamp not fully lit
never through the veil will I see,
as original intentions to be.

I dream of truth and beauty
yet principalities threaten,
and there is only nature of shadow.
It strikes against all strength of will
giving doubt, not hope.
It lurks in semi-darkness
existing in self deception –
Media, our periodical purpose
so misleads ...

Lift the veil from inside –
let the light shine from within!
Let Grace have its say and
know the hope of love, not doubt.

Our spirit is fed not by fear
but by greater reality, heaven made.
If we allow that from outside
to define our value within,
then purpose becomes tangled,
folded, confused, deluded ...
It hides value in the obscure.

Are my dreams of truth
or of darkness?
Will we clearly see?

November 24, 2020 Kill Devil Hills NC

Sometime in Early AM

Sometime in early AM ...
Room full of darkness,
centered by candle of light,
yet to be future desire
that would seed focus of hope.
Now, not seen or heard,
anticipation ...
Savior never said
the darkness would be slight,
that darkness of creative might
so governed by principalities
and power desire.
He never said it to be
easily held at distant bay.
Nor that it would understand
that center candle of light.
Control of soul, so seen in spirits dashed –
brings acrid winds of change
and charge to incite this flame,
this flame of hope and peaceful dreams.
So curse not that great darkness,
but light one candle, our only resolve.
Resist great principalities
and become that small mustard seed;
Refuse this Politic –
This Power Politic of greed!

November 3, 2020 Outer Banks NC

Rumble

Collective shudder,
a rumble of national proportion,
awakes me from deep sleep.
Three AM, a time for rest
and blissful respite,
disturbed by energy aligned.
Events, past present future
occlude all available reality,
and *Awareness Gestalt*.

Movements unknown
appropriate majority collective.
Shadow lands draw near
with each national breath;
A darkness that cannot be defined
yet defiles thoughts, words and actions,
shapes awareness unknown to self.

Anxiety waves, like ocean
upon darkness that seems light,
spring forth in projection-electron.
So passive seeming, yet,
each pass becomes hopeless;
in process, a hammer of doubt,
yet to be determined.

Talking, shouting, whispering heads,
empty in rhetorical undertaking
become subject, nihilistic –
Medium is the message, a non-choice,
Echoes of empty prophets ...
Thoughts of vapid nature
impose upon all who watch
but do not see.

Day sleepers awake,
find strength in faith not tested!
Pray for those yet oppressed,
Who dare to mention doubts,
Who dare to see with centered presence!
Only choice moral, given freely,
becomes collective action uncrossed.
Hold tight to the transcendent –
Reach out as it passes
the awareness of our
Collective Rumble.

November 2, 2020   Outer Banks NC

If We Seek Justice

If we seek justice, vengeance is not our path
If we seek non-violence, malice cannot live
If we seek peace, anger cannot prevail
If we seek enlightenment, darkness only shrouds
If we seek wisdom, prejudice is loss –
much excused by false hope and action.

"In love there is not hate,"
spoken by prophet forgotten.
Hysterical-historical, his words fall
on eyes, ears, and hearts closed.
If we seek truth, transparency is purpose.
If we speak truth, bias cannot present
untruths and shadow corollaries.

A path of hatred feeds itself
A path of violence begets itself
A path of darkness only blinds
and does not release, but only binds.
Healing the path, to forgive is to love,
compassion the key to guide us in light;
Ever present it shines in darkness' plain sight.

Look well that we may see
that small flame of hope,
not quite understood by
blindness to be.

To live and thrive
Our path is to love
Our wisdom forgiveness
Our beliefs respectful
from gifts above.
So walk while there's light
before darkness yet seen.
Hide not that understanding
but let it be bright.

May we heal this race now
in faith's hope and light ...
To this essence conceived
our heart's now full,
grant us new sight.

January 9, 2021 Kill Devil Hills NC

Principalities

Copters Cowling Carousel
in helix of Principalities,
Three giant birds, soaring swooping
shells of darkness patterns practice
landing rights to define ...
Judgment of nations prescribing
refinements motion potential.
Pretexts posed perceptions perpetual
justify, edify, indemnify –
This notion fading our humanity
in pretense of Righteousness, godly.

Waves of power, darkness,
momentarily wash my resistance
invisible to prophecies foretold.
Rotors thumping, senses numbing,
my inner threads of being
vibrate wildly in thunderous veil.
Connection with Presence eternal
is for this moment delayed, yet –
springs back with greater force.
In confusion, disbelief, indignation,
I don an armor of faith and watch
as a sleeper awakened.

Two birds in feinting frenzy
double back in contexts unknown.
Within the other, truth flies not;
A presidential principality,
existing not of flesh and blood
but an electron image seen nightly,
landing near the House of White
our lamp of patriotic purpose.

My question rolls
from nerve endings frayed,
can man survive this present state?
From violence comes the answer not,
faith's light hope is never late;
To hope is to love
and to love we are free,
choosing not the path
of sacred principalities.

February 2, 1991 Washington DC

One Thousand Cuts

One thousand cuts,
an array of secular wounds
To faith yet uncentered,
but under attack.
A belief in the divine
becomes not a spiritual journey,
but one of Politic.
A right of assembly
A right of expression
A right to believe as heart dictates.
A Right to share God-centered faith,
From Christian or Jew, taken –
A conquest of correctness political.
The divine within,
sacred texts, no longer.
A pinnacle of faith dictates,
Atheism is OK;
Just follow one's conscience.
Yea, con-science,
base secular,
another Political con.
Another cut, one thousandth.
A study of "correctical" thinking
again, informed by Politic.

A closing of Assembly Spiritual,
Yet purchase of "Alt-Spirit,"
Acceptable.
Thought police are searching,
expressions public and private,
deleterious to "The Public Good."
More cuts of one thousand.
Information altered,
shaped for power-centered control.
Control of speech
Control of movement
Control of life essence
Control of commerce
Control of all.

Death by One Thousand Cuts ...

November 3, 2020   Outer Banks NC

In Fear's Shadow

Covered light opaque,
A spiritual creative flat-line,
Loss not yet definable, but ongoing.
Swirling emptiness within.
Subconscious desire to lash out,
But where?

Are we in downward spiral,
or a new pattern of spiritual resource?
Within creator's silence is
this desert path, temptation filled.

Temptation to doubt
Temptation to fear
Temptation to hate
Love's essence and hope yet,
an unheard sacramental call.
A Pandemic of spirit,
endemic of loss.

I silently cry yet do not perceive.
my prayer Lord,
is that you understand.
That you know what I cannot.

May your light shine,
breaking through the opaque;
Grant us strength to see.

September 26, 2020   Outer Banks NC

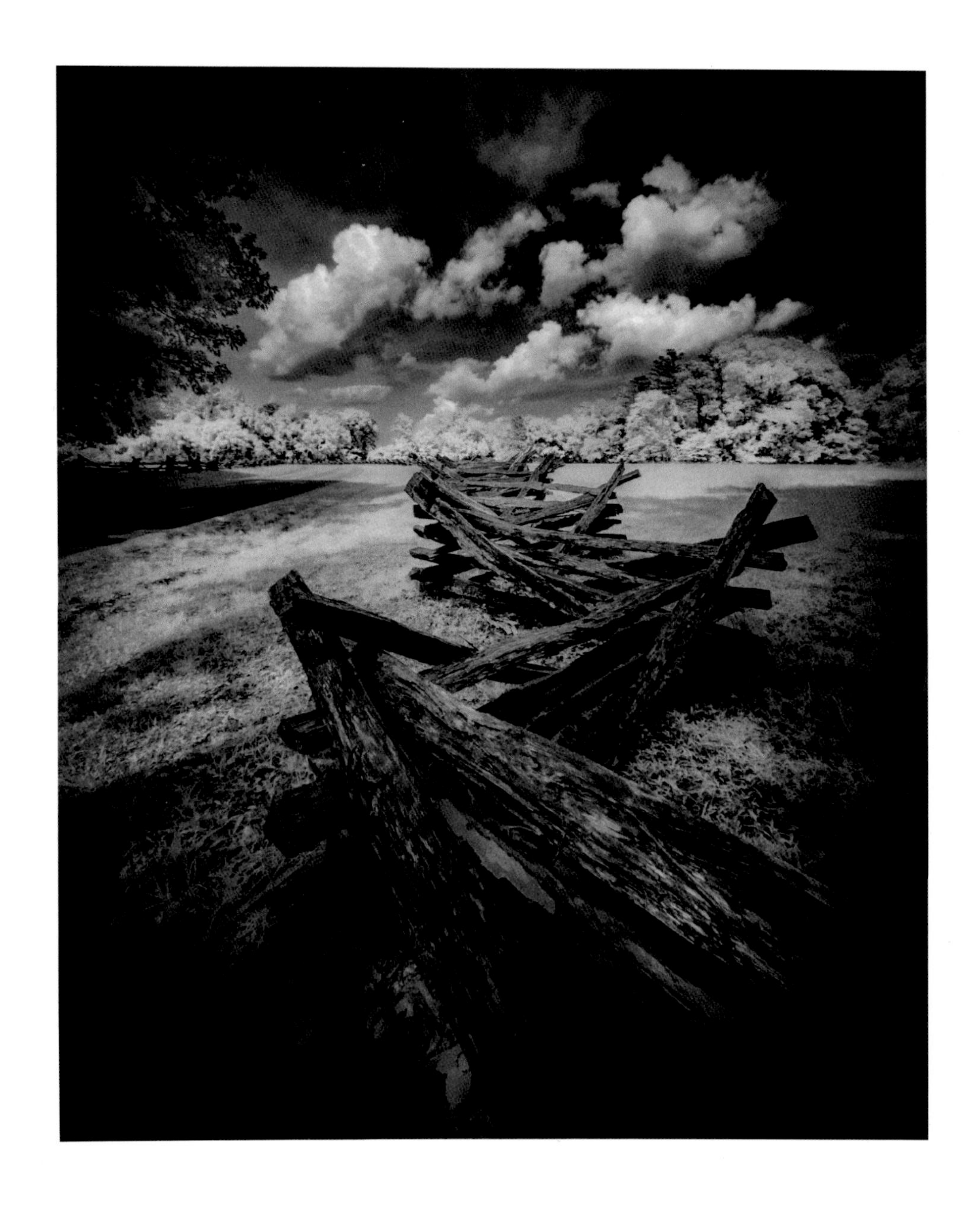

Standing at Attention

Are we present to available reality?

Flowing Cross

Cross flowing in motion
arches upward in faith,
Daily journey transition,
we ascend to a call.

Motion, cross crucial,
Increasing, releasing,
transcendent-translucent,
to light vision found.
Psyche transfigured
to the divine within
the heart moves outward
to those least ones bound;

Who thirsted for springs
Who hungered for life
Who shivered in darkness
Who ill needed care ...

Faith called to action
to know is to love.
Our zenith the potential
of possibilities found.

Christ placed one Body,
Communion of spirit
Cross flowing in motion –
A sacramental call!

November 27, 1990 Washington DC

Future Past

Pain future past,
an imperfect tense.
Empty fears consume
a space unscented
in spirit's disarray.

Alice, whirlwind, stop!
Your many doors confuse.
Seize this moment,
there's much to lose.
Another comes tomorrow,
but this again may never be...

1985 Nashville NC

God's Light on Fall Field

God's first morning light
illuminating open fields,
becomes a celebration of life;
colors glisten and reflect His love.
Doubts of evening past
like mist from morning vapor,
vanish as grace and truth
take fear's power away.

Searching for light eternal
to shine from within,
Fall field, brightly turning,
guides me through darkness present.
A granting of peace,
A respite from self doubt –
God's light on fall field,
Heals my spirit with love.

October 1988   Pennsylvania

Light Transcendent

I dream not of a thousand points
but one, that shines in darkness present.
A light of hope
A light of peace
That binds and does not loose.
A light of community
A light of faith
That affirms our calling to love.
A light eternal
A light to be
That illumines those least ones free.
A light transcendent
A light within,
That shines for all to see.

February 14, 1991   Washington DC

Morning's Sunset

Into morning's sunset
beyond castle walls,
my passions fly
upon wings of fantasy.
Between the cracks
of dark night's spell,
a silent truth longs
for faith's caress.

My awakening, this
hopeful envoy of heaven's
gate, leads me
through still shadows
to emerge in light's breath.
Scented of sweet
affirmations,
this melody sings
praise of life
and love eternal.

August 12, 1991 Washington DC

Scarlet Sunrise

Prayer of Life and Love

Unseen power, beyond awareness,
guiding, nurturing gifts eternal,
Your Spirit fills me with gentle strength.
You bring me to light in unseen places,
shielding me from darkness.

Let my faith equal your abounding love,
continue guiding me with loving hands.
I see only glimpses of your power
as it guides me in a blessed path.
Lord, I give you praise of life and love!

September 1988   Washington DC

Resonance

In motion flowing
like lute strings bound,
Images of spirit through
His will resound.
A varied pallet
these overtones paint,
like a fresco of faith –
God's many blessings found.

Outward to Spirit
each note complete,
Sound, beauty physical –
Returns, essence replete.
Not held or measured,
transparency increased,
It flows like a gentle breeze
whispering a Song of Peace.

August 13, 1990   Washington DC

White Wisps Dancing

Dawn creeps into window
pink cool and blue.
A call to ascend hard mountain,
changing through
to purpose mindful ...
Senses awake!

Upon my spirit,
the morning sun breaks.
Wisps of clouds white
upon aqua sky brush,
Pink slivers flowing
from horizon seeping, rush ...

Tree line dark green,
purple hues sublime,
Reality or Shadow,
within these, exist time?
Tomorrow's concerns
to clouds weeping, melt.

Tears, not from sadness
but from joy centered within;
This love lift cares away,
to white wisps dancing –
Lord, I live this day!

October 1990   Shrinemont VA

Tennessee Sunrise

Vapor's Silence

My tears dry
in vapor's silence
as soundless drops
in ocean's emptiness.
Within this essence
primal,
a seamless faith
draws near.

I am enveloped in darkness.

From shadows
that are light,
a desert voice
faintly cries –
Release, let go.

In love
there is not fear.

July 7, 1991 Somewhere on Planet Earth

Gordon Kreplin is a concert artist, teacher and photographer. He sees photography, music and language as one gift, an expression of a greater consciousness. Throughout his development as a musician, his studies and performances have taken him to Spain, South America, Portugal and the United States. He has always traveled with a camera to capture images that speak of melody, rhythm and form; his poetry is often a metaphor for those images.

He lives on the Outer Banks of North Carolina with his wife Cathy and their two cats, and with occasional visitations from grandchildren.

There are many who have been a support in his development as an artist. Fr. Ward Courtney, who guided him through difficult teenage years; John Bodnar, his first college English composition teacher; John Marlow, his first and most influential professor of guitar at American University; Evelyn Hayes, pianist, a compassionate and caring professor and coach who encouraged him to embrace a life of intense passion for music; Maestro José Tomás, professor of guitar at Óscar Esplá Conservatory in Alicante Spain, with whom Gordon studied for two years and found inspiration for a lifetime; his father, who made possible a wonderful college and post graduate experience in Spain; and, the community at St. Anselm's Abbey in Washington DC, where Gordon became an Oblate of St. Benedict.

And He said, as would only the Alpha and the Omega,
before passing through this veil of earthly reality,

"Love one another, as I have loved you."